Holiday Magic Books

Thanksgiving
MAGIC

by James W. Baker
pictures by George Overlie

Lerner Publications Company   Minneapolis

To my late father, Otis Fletcher Baker, to whom I will always be thankful for launching me into a lifelong fascination with magic when he returned home from a convention and gave me my first magical effect—a penny-in-the-box trick—which I still perform.

Copyright © 1989 by Lerner Publications Company

Library of Congress Cataloging-in-Publication Data

Baker, James W., 1926-
  Thanksgiving magic/by James W. Baker; pictures by George Overlie.
    p.   cm.—(Holiday magic books)
  Summary: Describes how to perform magic tricks with a
Thanksgiving theme.
  ISBN 0-8225-2233-0 (lib. bdg.)
  1. Tricks—Juvenile literature. 2. Thanksgiving Day—Juvenile
literature.   [1. Magic tricks. 2. Thanksgiving Day.]   I. Overlie,
George, ill. II. Title. III. Series: Baker, James W., 1926-
Holiday magic books.
GV1548.B345   1989
793.8—dc19   88-8310
                                                       CIP
                                                        AC

Manufactured in the United States of America

  2 3 4 5 6 7 8 9 10 98 97 96 95 94 93 92 91 90

CONTENTS

6

INTRODUCTION

Ever since the Pilgrims came to the New World and were helped by Native Americans, people in North America have come together each autumn to give thanks for a successful harvest. People may travel across the country to be with their families, or they may cross the street to celebrate with friends. Then they roast a turkey, bake apple and pumpkin pies, and pile their plates with dressing, potatoes, cranberry sauce, and other foods for a great feast.

After the feasting, you can entertain your friends and family—especially the ones who have spent the day cooking—by performing these magic tricks. With this cornucopia of Thanksgiving magic tricks, you can create a feast of fun for everyone!

A TURKEY TURNOVER

HOW IT LOOKS

Show your audience a piece of paper with some Thanksgiving turkeys drawn on it. Fold the paper in a certain way and then unfold it. The turkeys have magically turned upside down.

8

For this trick, you will need a piece of paper, about 8 x 2½ inches (20 x 6 cm). Draw some turkeys on the paper as shown (**Figure 1**).

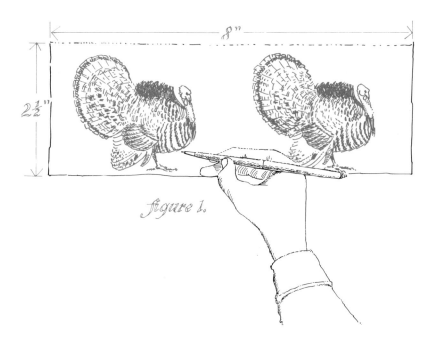

figure 1.

1. Hold the drawing between your thumbs and forefingers, facing your friend (**Figure 2**).

audience viewpoint
figure 2.

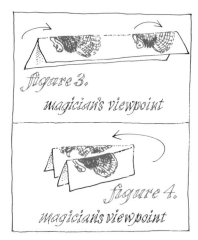

figure 3.
magician's viewpoint

figure 4.
magician's viewpoint

2. Fold the top half down toward you (**Figure 3**).

3. Fold the right end to the left, away from you (**Figure 4**). Do the same again (**Figure 5**).

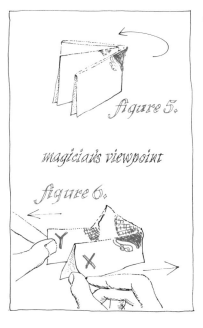

figure 5.

magician's viewpoint

figure 6.

4. Unfold the paper by taking the corner closest to you, "X" by the right thumb and forefinger and the inside corner, "Y" with the left thumb and forefinger (**Figure 6**).

5. Draw your hands apart, stretching the paper out between your hands (**Figure 7**) and lift the front half of the paper upward. The picture will have magically turned upside down.

figure 7.

11

FINDING THANKSGIVING

HOW IT LOOKS

Hand out six or seven pieces of paper to several people in the audience. Explain that you are going to do some Thanksgiving magic. Ask one person to write "Thanksgiving" on her slip of paper and hand it to you. Crumple the paper into a ball and toss it into an empty paper bag.

Now ask the others, one by one, to write a holiday other than Thanksgiving on a slip of paper and hand the paper to you. As each one does this, crumple the paper into a ball and toss it into the bag. Shake the bag and mix up the balls of paper. Reach into the bag and take out the balls one by one, holding each one to your forehead. When you come to the slip with "Thanksgiving" written on it, tell the audience you have found it. Unfold the paper and show the audience you are correct.

ball bearing

HOW TO MAKE IT

For this trick, you will need six or seven small pieces of paper, a pencil, a paper bag, and a small metal ball bearing, which you conceal in your right hand.

1. Give pieces of paper to six or seven members of the audience. Ask one person to write "Thanksgiving" on her slip of paper and hand it to you. As you wad the paper into a ball, secretly roll the ball bearing inside it.

2. Wad the other pieces of paper the same way, but without ball bearings inside. The Thanksgiving slip is heavier and you will know it by its weight when you hold the wad to your forehead.

3. As you open the Thanksgiving slip, let the hidden ball bearing roll into your hand, unseen by the audience.

4. Pocket the ball bearing while members of the audience are checking the slip of paper to see if you are right.

SIX
PUMPKIN
PIES

As you arrange six pumpkin pies on the table, tell your friend something like, "My grandma made six pumpkin pies for Thanksgiving and arranged them in a cross." Place them so there are four pies in one line and three pies in the other. Continue with, "She challenged me to rearrange the pies so that there were four in each line, and since I am a magician, I could do it. Can you?" Chances are your friend won't be able to do it. You show him how.

HOW TO MAKE IT

From construction paper, make six silver-dollar-size disks that look like pumpkin pies.

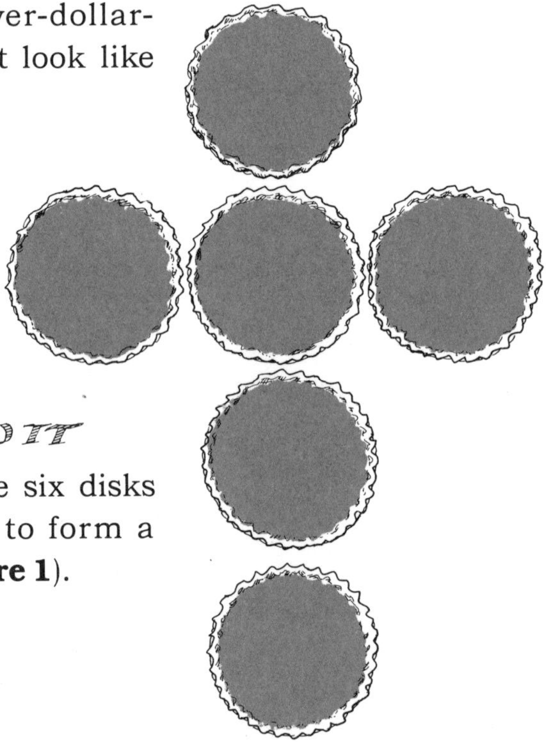

figure 1.

HOW TO DO IT

1. Arrange the six disks on a table to form a cross (**Figure 1**).

2. Challenge your friend to rearrange the pies so that they will total four both ways.

3. When your friend gives up, you simply pick up the disk at the bottom of the cross and place it on top of the disk in the middle of the cross (**Figure 2**).

figure 2.

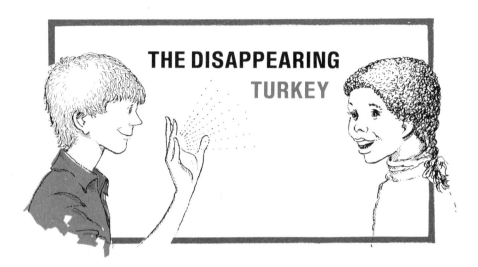

THE DISAPPEARING
TURKEY

HOW IT LOOKS

Ask your friend if she has ever noticed how fast a turkey disappears on Thanksgiving Day and offer to illustrate what you mean by magic. Rub a small cardboard disk, with a picture of a turkey on both sides, on your left arm just above your elbow. The disk with the picture of the turkey vanishes completely, just like a real turkey does on Thanksgiving Day.

1. Cut a round disk about the size of a quarter from a piece of plain cardboard. Draw a picture of a turkey on both sides of the cardboard disk (**Figure 1**).
2. You will need to be wearing a shirt with a collar.

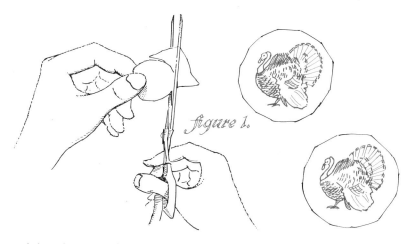

figure 1.

1. Show your friend the cardboard disk with a picture of a turkey on both sides.

2. With your sleeves rolled up, bend your left arm so that your left hand is beside your left cheek. Place your left elbow on the table (**Figure 2**).

3. Pick up the disk with your right hand and rub it on your left arm just above your left elbow (**Figure 3**).

figure 2.

figure 3.

4. Drop the disk on the table—supposedly by accident—and pick it up in your left hand, transferring it to your right hand and begin rubbing it on your arm again, just as before.

5. Once again drop the disk—accidentally again—on the table. Pick up the disk again with your left hand. Pretend to transfer it to your right hand, but keep it in your left hand. Rub your left arm with your right hand as before, holding your hand to look like the disk is still there.

6. While your left hand—secretly holding the disk—is by your left cheek, slip the disk into your collar.

7. Attention is still focused on your right hand (empty) as you pretend to rub the disk against your arm just above your left elbow. Lift your right hand, spread your fingers and show that the turkey disk has vanished like the real turkey on Thanksgiving Day.

THE PILGRIM'S HAT AND THE TURKEY

HOW IT LOOKS

You show the audience two index cards. A picture of a pilgrim's hat is on one and a picture of a roasted turkey is on the other. Cover the two pictures with a handkerchief. Then remove the picture of the pilgrim's hat and put it in your back pocket. Say the magic word, "cranberry." The two pictures have magically changed places. The pilgrim's hat is under the handkerchief and the turkey is in your pocket.

HOW TO MAKE IT

For this trick, you will need three index cards. On one card, draw a pilgrim's hat and on another, draw a roasted turkey. On the third card, the trick card, draw a pilgrim's hat on one side and a roasted turkey on the other (**Figure 1**). Both pictures of a pilgrim's hat and both pictures of a roasted turkey should look exactly alike. You will also need a handkerchief.

figure 1.

other side blank

other side blank

pilgrim hat on reverse side

trick card

23

1. Before you begin, place the turkey card in your back pocket. The audience doesn't know it is there.

2. Hold the pilgrim's hat card and the trick card in your left hand and show them to the audience. Make sure the turkey on the trick card is facing the audience. Don't let anyone see the backs of the cards.

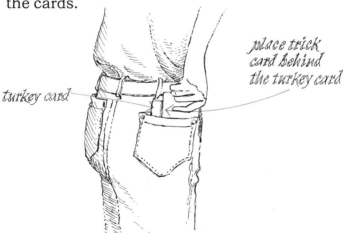

turkey card

place trick card behind the turkey card

3. Cover the two cards with the handkerchief.

4. Reach under the handkerchief and take the trick card in your right hand. Turn it around so the pilgrim's hat is facing the audience. Take this card out from under the handkerchief and hold it up so the audience can see it is the pilgrim's hat.

5. Place the card in your pocket *behind* the turkey card that is already there. Now say the magic word, "cranberry."

6. Remove the handkerchief and the audience will see that the pilgrim's hat card, which they saw you put in your pocket, is magically back in your hand.

7. Reach in your pocket and remove the turkey card, which is in *front*. The two cards have magically changed places. The trick card—with pictures on both sides—remains safely out of sight in your pocket.

THE TURKEY AND THE GUN

HOW IT LOOKS

Tell a story something like "A hunter picked up his gun and went out to shoot a turkey." Show the audience an 8-inch (20-cm) square piece of thin paper divided into sixteen 2-inch (5-cm) squares. Eight of the squares are marked with a "T" for "turkey." The other eight squares are marked with a "G" for "gun." Fold the paper and then make a cut with a heavy pair of scissors. Unfold the paper and show what happened: the "gun" squares are all separate while the "turkey" squares are all joined together in one piece. "The gun has exploded and broken into eight pieces while the turkey, still in one piece, escaped with his life and will not grace a Thanksgiving dinner table this year."

1. Cut a square, 8 x 8 inches (20 x 20 cm), from a sheet of onionskin or tissue paper.
2. Using a ruler and a pencil, divide the paper into exact 2-inch (5-cm) squares. Then, with a wide felt-tip pen, write "T" and "G" in the squares exactly as shown (**Figure 1**).

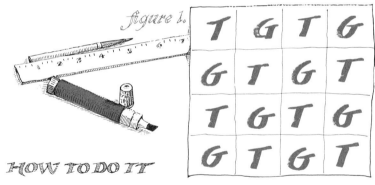

figure 1.

1. Tell the story from the section on HOW IT LOOKS and show the audience the piece of paper with alternating "T's" and "G's." Explain that "T" stands for "turkey" and "G" stands for "gun."

2. Follow the directions exactly as stated:

A. Fold the upper portion forward and down, making a crease through the center of the second row from top (**Figure 2**).

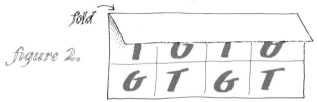

figure 2.

fold

B. Fold the lower portion backward and up, making a crease through the center of the second row from the bottom (**Figure 3**).

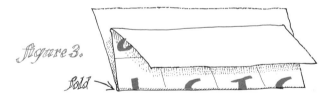

figure 3.

fold

C. Fold the right side forward and to the left, creasing the center of the second row from the right (**Figure 4**).

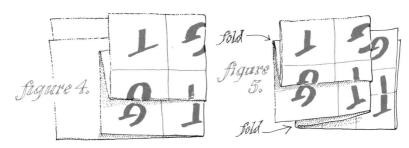

D. Fold the left side backward and to the right, creasing the center of the second row from the left (**Figure 5**).

E. You now have a square, which you fold diagonally to form a triangle (**Figure 6**).

F. Fold the triangle in half to form a smaller triangle (**Figure 7**).

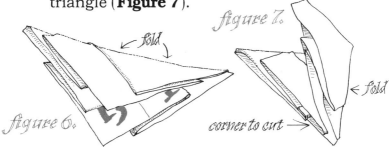

29

3. Cut off the corner of the triangle that was folded last, the corner with the big fold. (**Figure 8**).

4. When the cut pieces of paper are unfolded, your friend will see that the "G's" (the gun) have come apart in eight pieces while the "T's" (the turkey) are linked together in one piece (**Figure 9**). The gun has broken apart and the turkey has escaped in one piece.

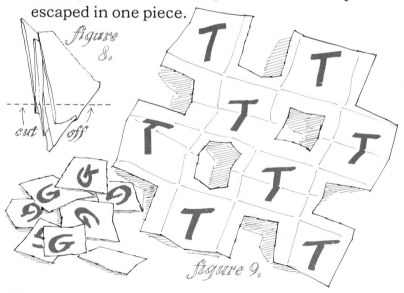

figure 8.

cut off

figure 9.

HOW IT LOOKS

Show three small shipping tags to your audience. On one is a picture of a roasted turkey, one a picture of a hot dog, and one a picture of a hamburger. Ask a volunteer from the audience to mix up the three tags and hand you all three behind your back so you can't see them. With the tags behind you and without looking, drop two of them on the floor, keeping the other one in your hand. Since you are doing Thanksgiving magic, it is always the turkey tag left in your hand and never the tags with the hot dog or hamburger pictures.

HOW TO MAKE IT

1. Draw a turkey on one shipping tag, a hot dog on another, and a hamburger on a third.
2. Force a knife blade under the *upper* half of the gummed reinforcement on the hot dog tag. On the hamburger tag in a similar manner loosen the *lower* half of the reinforcement. On the turkey tag, leave the reinforcement as it is, firmly stuck down (**Figure 1**).

firmly stuck down   *top half loose*   *bottom half loose*

figure 1.

1. After you've shown the audience the three tags, ask a volunteer to mix up the tags and hand them to you behind your back so you can't see them.

2. Feel the gummed reinforcements with your finger nail. You will easily be able to tell which are the hot dog and hamburger tags because the reinforcements will be a little loose. Drop these on the floor.

3. Before you show the audience the tag left in your hand, tell them that you always keep the turkey because this is Thanksgiving magic.

THANKSGIVING LEFTOVERS

HOW IT LOOKS

Toss three tiny balls of paper onto the table, saying that they represent Thanksgiving leftovers. Pick up one paper ball and place it into your left hand, saying you're putting one leftover into the refrigerator. Do the same with the second paper ball, saying you're putting another leftover in the refrigerator. Pick up the third paper ball the same way and say you are going to eat it, placing it not in your hand but in your pocket.

Open your left hand (the refrigerator) and out roll all three of the paper balls (leftovers). Tell the audience that it is always difficult to get rid of Thanksgiving leftovers. Repeat the trick several times, putting two leftovers in the refrigerator (your left hand) and one in your pocket (supposedly to eat) only to have three pop up again in the refrigerator (your left hand).

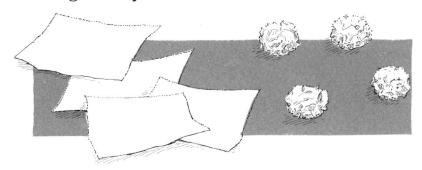

HOW TO MAKE IT

For this trick, you will need to make *four* tiny paper balls by wadding up small pieces of paper. All four should look alike.

1. Toss three paper balls onto the table, telling the audience that they represent Thanksgiving leftovers.

2. The fourth paper ball is hidden in your right hand (**Figure 1**). The natural bend of your fingers hides it without raising suspicion.

3. Pick up one paper ball between your right thumb and forefinger and place it into your half-closed left fist (**Figure 2**).

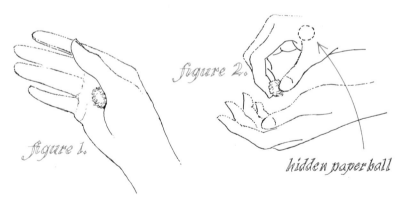

figure 2.

figure 1.

hidden paper ball

4. Pick up the second paper ball from the table and place it into your half-closed left fist. At the same time, drop the other ball hidden in your right hand into your left. At this point you have three balls in your left hand but the audience thinks there are only two.

5. Pick up the third ball from the table and *pretend* to put it in your pocket, saying this is the leftover to be eaten. Actually, you bring the ball back out of your pocket in your partly closed right hand. Thus you are ready to repeat the trick with one ball secretly in your right hand.

6. Open your left hand fully and let all 3 balls drop out onto the table, showing that it is indeed hard to get rid of Thanksgiving leftovers.

7. Repeat the trick a few times to prove your point.

THE PROFESSOR KNOWS

Show the audience pictures of foods that are often served at Thanksgiving: turkey, dressing, cranberry sauce, sweet potatoes, pumpkin pie, and biscuits. Have a volunteer from the audience point to one of the pictures. Tell the audience that you know a professor who is a mental telepathist. If the volunteer brings her into the room, she will be able to name the food the volunteer chose, without seeing the pictures. The volunteer brings the professor into the room. She immediately names the food that was chosen.

HOW TO MAKE IT

1. For this trick, you can either draw the pictures or cut them out of a magazine and paste them on index cards.
2. You will also need a friend to act as a professor.
3. Ahead of time, you and your friend need to work out a code in which the first letter in each professor's name is the same as the first letter in each kind of food. For example:

> Professor Thomas = turkey
> Professor Daniels = dressing
> Professor Chambers = cranberry sauce
> Professor Swinson = sweet potatoes
> Professor Peters = pumpkin pie
> Professor Bradford = biscuits

1. When you're ready to perform, lay the separate pictures out on a table. Have a volunteer point to a food, without naming it out loud, but so the entire audience can see what he chose.
2. Tell the volunteer to go into another room to get Professor so-and-so. Give a different name depending on the food chosen, according to your code.
3. Turn over the pictures and put them in a pile.
4. When your friend comes into the room, she will know which food was chosen by the name of the professor that the volunteer asked for. All she has to do is to put on a good mental telepathist act and dramatically announce the food that was chosen.

A MAGICAL THANKSGIVING TURKEY

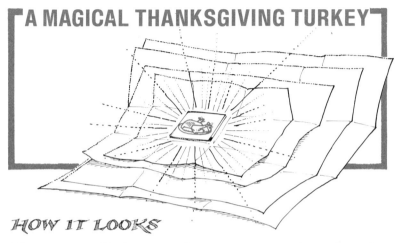

HOW IT LOOKS

Place a small picture of an empty serving plate in the center of a square of red paper and fold the edges over it. Fold a green sheet around the red packet, and then fold a yellow sheet around the green packet. Finally, fold a blue sheet around the yellow packet. Say the magic word, "cranberry," and unfold all the packets. Inside is a picture of a serving plate which is no longer empty. It now holds a roasted turkey that you have magically produced.

1. For this trick, you will need seven sheets of paper: two identical red sheets 5 x 5 inches (12.5 x 12.5 cm), two identical green sheets 6 x 6 inches (15 x 15 cm), two identical yellow sheets 7 x 7 inches (17.5 x 17.5 cm), and one blue sheet 8 x 8 inches (20 x 20 cm).

2. Triple fold all seven sheets both ways (**Figure 1**). After you've creased the papers, unfold them so they're flat again.

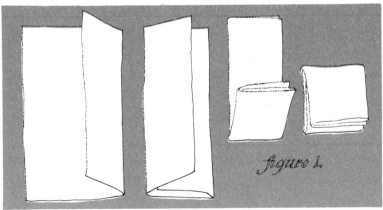

figure 1.

3. On one piece of cardboard, 1½ inches (4 cm) square, draw a picture of a serving plate holding a roasted turkey. On another, draw a picture of an empty serving plate (**Figure 2**).

figure 2.

4. Place the picture of the serving plate with the turkey in the center of one of the red sheets and fold the sheet along the creases. Place the folded red sheet in the center of one of the green sheets and fold the green sheet. Place the folded green sheet in the center of one of the yellow sheets and fold the yellow sheet.

5. Turn the yellow packet over, opening side down, and paste the second yellow sheet over it, back to back, so the openings face out. Fold the second yellow sheet around the second green sheet, which is folded around the second red sheet.

6. Place the entire pasted-together yellow packet in the center of the single sheet of blue paper, making sure the red sheet without the picture in it is facing up, and fold the blue sheet around the yellow packet.

1. Show the folded packet to your friend. Unfold the blue sheet, then the yellow sheet, then the green sheet, and finally the red sheet (**Figure 3**).

2. Show your friend the small piece of cardboard with the picture of the empty serving plate on it. Place it in the center of the red sheet.

3. Fold up the red sheet, then the green around the red, and then the yellow around the green.

4. At this point you must distract your friend. Look him directly in the eye and say, "Were you sure that plate was empty?" At that moment, turn the yellow packet over, place it in the blue sheet, and fold the blue sheet around the yellow packet.

5. Say the magic word, "cranberry," and open the packets one at a time. When you reach the red packet, it contains a picture of a plate with a roasted turkey on it. You have magically produced a Thanksgiving turkey.

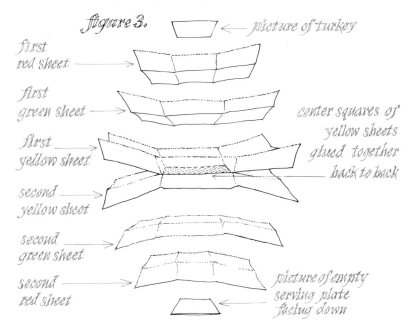

figure 3.

picture of turkey

first red sheet

first green sheet

first yellow sheet

second yellow sheet

center squares of yellow sheets glued together back to back

second green sheet

second red sheet

picture of empty serving plate facing down

TRICKS FOR BETTER MAGIC

Here are some simple rules you should keep in mind while learning to perform the tricks in this book.

1. Read the entire trick several times until you thoroughly understand it.
2. Practice the trick alone or in front of a mirror until you feel comfortable doing the trick, then present it to an audience.
3. Learn to perform one trick perfectly before moving on to another trick. It is better to perform one trick well than a half dozen poorly.
4. Work on your "presentation." Make up special "patter" (what you say while doing a trick) that is funny and entertaining. Even the simplest trick becomes magical when it is properly presented.
5. Choose tricks that suit you and your personality. Some tricks will work better for you than others.

Stick with these. *Every* trick is not meant to be performed by *every* magician.

6. Feel free to experiment and change a trick to suit you and your unique personality so that you are more comfortable presenting it.

7. Never reveal the secret of the trick. Your audience will respect you much more if you do not explain the trick. When asked how you did a trick, simply say "by magic."

8. Never repeat a trick for the same audience. If you do, you will have lost the element of surprise and your audience will probably figure out how you did it the second time around.

9. Take your magic seriously, but not yourself. Have fun with magic and your audience will have fun along with you.

ABOUT THE AUTHOR

James W. Baker, a magician for over 30 years, has performed as "Mister Mystic" in hospitals, orphanages, and schools around the world. He is a member of the International Brotherhood of Magicians and the Society of American Magicians, and is author of *Illusions Illustrated*, a magic book for young performers.

From 1951 to 1963, Baker was a reporter for *The Richmond (VA) News Leader*. From 1963 to 1983, he was an editor with the U.S. Information Agency, living in Washington, D.C., India, Turkey, Pakistan, the Philippines, and Tunisia, and traveling in 50 other countries. Today Baker and his wife, Elaine, live in Williamsburg, Virginia, where he performs magic and writes for the local newspaper, *The Virginia Gazette*.

ABOUT THE ARTIST

George Overlie is a talented artist who has illustrated numerous books. Born in the small town of Rose Creek, Minnesota, Overlie graduated from the New York Phoenix School of Design and began his career as a layout artist. He soon turned to book illustration and proved his skill and versatility in this demanding field. For Overlie, fantasy, illusion, and magic are all facets of illustration and have made doing the Holiday Magic books a real delight.